MyOTHER TONGUE

FUTUREPOEM BOOKS
NEW YORK CITY
2017

MyOTHER TONGUE

ROSA ALCALÁ

ISBN: 978-0-9960025-5-4

FIRST EDITION | FIRST PRINTING

This edition first published in paperback by Futurepoem books
P.O. Box 7687 JAF Station, NY, NY 10116
www.futurepoem.com

Executive Editor: Dan Machlin
Managing Editor: Carly Dashiell
Books Editor: Ted Dodson
Guest Editors: Mei-mei Berssenbrugge and Roberto Tejada

Cover design: Everything Studio (www.everythingstudio.com)
Interior design: Nikkita Cohoon (www.nikkita.co)
Typefaces: Sabon (text and titles)

Printed in the United States of America on acid-free paper

This project is supported in part by the New York State Council on the Arts with
the support of Governor Andrew Cuomo and the New York State Legislature, and
by public funds from the The New York City Department of Cultural Affairs in
partnership with the City Council. Futurepoem books is also supported in part
by The Leaves of Grass Fund and The New York Community Trust. Futurepoem
books is the publishing program of Futurepoem, Inc., a New York state-based
501(c)3 non-profit organization dedicated to creating a greater public awareness
and appreciation of innovative literature.

Distributed to the trade by Small Press Distribution, Berkeley, California
Toll-free number (U.S. only): 800.869.7553
Bay Area/International: 510.524.1668
orders@spdbooks.org
www.spdbooks.org

For María, my mother

To Raquel Inés, my daughter

CONTENTS

FOUR

A writer is someone who plays with his mother's body.

—Roland Barthes, *The Pleasure of the Text*,
translated by Richard Miller

Una grammatica fluía de la mamma:
la leche manando,
la lengua y el trans.

—Cecilia Vicuña, *i tu*

"As"—always t/here.   Is
unravel (h)ems of was/will
be(es), (h)is huhs, (h)er tongues.

—Tonya M. Foster, *A Swarm of Bees in High Court*

ONE

THE STORY TO BE WRITTEN

(For Farid Matuk)

To the archives
I have sent
your early hours
descending the
basement stairs—a line
   of jeans found there
       frozen overnight—then waiting
at The Rag Shop
for a ride
that would never come—your
   girlhood—your marriage—in my
      rearview—the beginning
and the end
       And at the machine
        —the vague
           answers—
            of what you did—between   The pictures
    cannot resolve
the stories
not told
—nor mine—to tell—
   although
       for the famous poet
        I dream-sign a copy
  of my book

  —a painting
    on a wedding chest
      —Cassone—
   depicting
     highlights
       each

         curse

This land, angular and strange—we are
citizens—
—our ascension—as Icarus
and then our
descent—the erased trail
 of migrants

With our skin
we hoped to touch
and worship
a new
belonging

 This agave, this aloe vera
   through which my nephew
      went tumbling
is where I live now—jagged
as this poem—
but also a poultice
 for the wounds

Sand blows
    the metaphor of the border
    into the mouths
        of women
        who walk daily
            between sovereignties
            to care
            for our children
            our homes

You came
to give your children
—a cliché—
    something
    to get them started—into breathing
I came fully into
my own
    and can
        barely
            kiss you
with these wavering
    words—you cannot
        —anyway—
            make them out
                    (reading glasses or
                        not)

The book opens
to your
distance   The phone
rings and rings—can

you reach it
amongst
things—
  the nubby

    orange

     suit you

      wore on

       the ship—

(cruised by expectations)

If leaving
isn't
my
legacy
what is—
  I wandered off
into a desert
of foreign species—the
 Mulberry's
  roots
  invading
  our mid-century house

The gypsy
with your
name in
Boston
asked
me if I
wanted
a reading
I said
I was
also there
for a
reading
and did she
want one
from
me—once a party girl—I now
                                        spend an afternoon
                                                    touring
                                                    rare manuscripts
                        and preening
for the ceiling, its carved figures and
white endowment   What I want?
to be housed there
to marry it

It might take the second
sinking
of the Titanic
        to allow me
                entry

The Gutenberg Bible
glows beneath
a glass case
    and a floor above
        I tremble among
        the stacks
of papers that
pierce
    draft to
        influence

At dinner in a fine
establishment
I make
everyone
sad
talking
of you—and
the desire
for the waiter—
Portuguese—becomes
    a second act

This
imminence
of grief
and the
description
of fresh
hake

O, Bull
in your white apron
I am not tricked out
in a cow suit
but in a sweater
dress
whose neck
cowls
from the
anecdote—my mother, it begins,
     I found in an archive   she was
          smiling among the photographs—
tuck me
dear waiter
in layers
of wine

The story to be
written—or—
this flight
this flight
this flight—from—
its
gravity

Big Donor—his fortune
in telescoping—says
it's really weak
you can loosen its pull
with a magnet

We have all in our heads
ancestral myths awaiting, even when
    freely
           our bodies move
                  away from them

My daughter's
first attempts:
"mama okay,"
"papa okay"
and "mess"

What likely
cost
incurred
as one
reads
or writes   What is
to be read to or by
strangers that
isn't meant
to be sold
or bought?

Mother,
forgive
me for
        wanting you to remain familiar
as I flirt with the waiter

—and for
　　my excursions:
a daughter
　　　　　　whose arranged marriage
　　　　　　　　is not with
　　　　　　　　　　Spanish

In the picture
　　next to the others
　　　　　　I am the shortest

No one knows
to pluck
tenderly
from the
folds of
your linen closet
the original
sheets
on which nothing
was
conceived

I say
it's an
injustice—the wine
　　　　coming over me—your face
　　　　　　and voice
splitting
me from
there:

"I walk
to the
store
when
they are
not
looking"—A dream
        that swings
                its legs
                        off the bed

A friend with no deeds
to these lands
said he worked when others
wrote—for his mother
her jewels stolen

        a citizenship
              fraught
                    in these acts
when in the writing
of them we enter
law, we strike
        our names—

the X in the dark
field
drawing
us through
blue lights

Signs to land us, others
to exit

By twos we enter
the story,
and leave the ark
built to survive
    the telling
        of catastrophes
                —one by
                    one—

MISSING

When it happened I camped out all night hoping to hear a leg drag from page to page, then I went in with all my gear and could barely breathe. I made it to love (n.), dug holes and inserted tubes, propped myself in a chair and promptly fell asleep. I dreamt of air going in and bubbles ascending from its depths. Finally, I closed its cover, attached wheels to it and pushed it from place to place. It has been like this ever since. Where she is, I'm not sure, but a lady she is not, among the fingers and gloves and slippers. A ghost of her perhaps in the servant and in the cloth. Some of it Greek, most of it lost. Plenary in volume, black ticking and muslin. At times I wear an entry and catch her scent. At the airport, I run my finger down words as if they were plumbers. What I need is a nanny to keep my child from crying. What I need is to stick to the task. She tripped and fell, my own mother, into the dictionary, precisely the week my tissue and blood wrote their own codex. It's amazing that with so many words at her disposal she hasn't sent me one. Why not make use of the key to utter a thing: myth machine anger. bull brute cry. bon as this azure. What are the sounds for but to hear what isn't there. An act of sliding, a waterproof coat, a spatula, a wedge to be driven. It's a given she's still living. You can tell by the crumbs she's left across definitions.

AT HOBBY LOBBY

She tosses a bolt of fabric into the air. Hill country, prairie, a horse trots there. I say three yards, and her eyes say more: What you need is guidance, a hand that can zip scissor through cloth. You need a picture of what you've lost. To double the width against the window for the gathering. Consider where you sit in the morning (transparency's appealing, except it blinds us before day's begun). How I long to captain that table, to repeat in a beautiful accent a customer's request. My mother cut threads from buttons with her teeth, inquiring with a finger in the band if it dug into the waist. Or kneeled against her client and pulled a hem down to a calf to cool a husband's collar. I can see this in my sleep, among notions. My bed was inches from the sewing machine, a dress on the chair weeping its luminescent frays. Sleep was the sound of insinuation, a zigzag to keep holes receptive. Or awakened by a backstitch balling under the foot. A needle cracking? Blood on a white suit? When my baby's asleep I write to no one and cannot expect a response. The fit's poor, always. No one wears it out the door. But fashions continue to fly out of magazines like girls out of windows. Sure, they are my sisters. Their machines, my own. The office from which I wave to them in their descent has uneven curtains, made with my own pink and fragile hands.

DEAR MARIA

Dear Mary, Mariah, Marie

Dear mamá, mamacita, and mami

Dear fourth wheel of the Trinity

Dear Puerto Rican Ingénue
                    in a Red Sash

Dear Off With Their Heads

Dear Diva

Dear Aria, missing its M (Dear Storage Engine)

Dear Ships in Your Name

Dear Asteroid
   discovered in 1877

Dear Song
            by
                    Café Tacuba
                    Green Day
                    The Jacksons
                    Men at Work
                    Blondie
                    Ricky Martin
                    Wu-Tang Clan
                        , et al.

Dear María, spoken in the bird's tail
of Papau New Guinea

"How do you solve a problem like Maria?"

Dear Pool Type Reactor

Dear Uranium How You Enrich Us

Dear Spanish Biscuit

Dear Sacrificial Virgins,
       of red or blond hair
       of dark brunette
       of the slip, apron, or veil, but never a hat
       of the fresh complexion turned composite
       of Jack the Ripper's complete works
       of fluency
              in Welsh
              Spanish
              English
              Quechua
              French

       of obscure and undocumented
              origins

                   and of las colonias
Querida María (de los Angeles
       de la Luz,
       de Jesús,
       del Refugio) walking home or waiting

for Transporte de Personal
without executive safe routes

Dear Señorita Maquiladora
Dexterous, tolerant of tedium
model workers
for Lexmark, FoxConn,
CommScope, etc.

Dear Queen of the Plasma TV and Print Cartridge

Dear Miss Stainless Steel Appliance

Dear Crowned with Cigarettes/Soda Cans/Boot Prints/
Dear Left without Nipples in the Desert Branded

Dear Virgen de Guadalupe,
hand us your sanitary napkin

Blessed art thou,
your blood is
on everything.

VOICE ACTIVATION

Do not forget that a poem, although it is composed in the language of information, is not used in the language-game of giving information.

—Ludwig Wittgenstein, *Zettel*, translated by G.E.M. Anscombe

This poem, on the other hand, is activated by the sound of my voice, and, luckily, I am a native speaker. Luckily, I have no accent and you can understand perfectly what I am saying to you via this poem. I have been working on this limpid voice, through which you can read each word as if rounded in my mouth, as if my tongue were pushing into my teeth, my lips meeting and jaws flexing, so that even if from birth you've been taught to read faces before words and words as faces, you'll feel not at all confused with what I say on the page. But maybe you'll see my name and feel a twinge of confusion. Have no doubt, my poem is innocent and transparent. So when I say, I think I'll make myself a sandwich, the poem does not say, I drink an isle of bad trips. Or if I say, my mother is dying, where is her phone. The poem does not say, try other it spying, spare us ur-foam. One way to ensure the poem and its reader no misunderstanding is to never modulate. I'm done with emotion, I'm done, especially with that certain weakness called exiting one's intention. What I mean is Spanish. What a mess that is, fishing for good old American bread and ending up with a boatload of uncles and their boxes of salt cod, a round of aunts poking for fat in your middle. So you see, Wittgenstein, even the sandwich isn't always made to my specifications; it's the poem that does what I demand. Everything else requires a series of steps. I call the nurse's station and explain to the nurse—her accent thick as thieves—that I'd like to speak to my mother. She calls out to my mother: "It's your daughter" (really, she says this in Spanish, but for the sake of voice activation and this poem, you understand I can't go there), and she hands the phone to my mother, and my mother, who is not the poem, has trouble understanding me. So I write this poem, which understands me perfectly and never needs the nurse's station and never worries about unintelligible accents or speaking loudly enough or the trouble with dying, which can be understood as a loss of language. If so, the immigrant, my mother, has been misunderstood for so long; this death is from her last interpreter.

HERITAGE SPEAKER

What good is it to erect
of absence
a word
like radiator
when we've vents
that expel heat
as air.

When I teach my daughter
to speak
and build a woman
out of me
that is not her mother
but some propriety.

A treason of simple
subjects, I never had use
in Spanish for the word
barn
and then
"woke up and a horse
was staring at me." (Joe Brainard)

Softly-pureed,
cooled, this diction dumb
in either
tongue. But what
is a mother's warmth
if not her wit?

Bernadette (Mayer) "turns to me
in the shower" and says
motherhood is now
fashionable among
the girl poets. If so, I want
my hat, a feather in it.
Mallarmé's, in fact.

TWO

MY BODY'S PRODUCTION

My body's
> a carder

>> a spinner

a crusher of blood seeds
> and milk-thread miller

loom of alveoli
> powered by rivers

Here you will find the frock for every vivid hour.

continuous din
> tiresome

>> to visitors

speedy and needy
> and frayed at the ends:

>>> piecers

>>>> & scavengers

>>>>> quick on the mend
>>>>> (those motherless creatures
>>>>> their tiny hands)

> and my operative, so tender: here's her
> portrait

with shuttle
            as scepter

My body it triggered
and pierced her
            left kidney

Q. You were perfectly straight and healthy before you worked in
   a mill?

A. Yes, I was as straight a little girl as ever went up and down town.

Q. Where are you now?

A. In the poorhouse.

And does my body regret
      what it has done?

I'm not responsible
      for its design

My body now weaves
a funeral shroud

      for mother
            her wooden gears
                  ground down

The last milk-threads
    unfold, from specter to form

    to be carried off
    to the dye house
        hot work
            for the men

Marriage
    to the doffer
        momentarily postponed.

*I do not dance so much for I cannot work so hard and dance
so much.*

OFFERING

Nestled
in the armpit
your head, my sweat

rocket fuel
baptism
from the deepest

layers of fat. A net
hurled at me
by the longshoremen

of public insult.
Radiant in parts
per million

retardant
of flames

my milk
I give to you
as once

I gave industry
an organ.

PURITY & DANGER: A PERFORMANCE

I lumbered across the stage
nothing for a costume
but a horse trapping
adorned with two figures:
a bird pecking a man's eyes
and a mother nursing.

In my arms a rooster,
an old tough hen. And when I made swift
with a knife the front row covered
their heads.

Three lovely dancers
rehearsed my once youthful gait
through blood.

Behind me a dream projected
of an old lover
wearing too big a shirt,
as if from the collar
the neck kept a distance.

A voice amplified asked:
    Do you want to kiss him?

No, I breathed into the microphone:
    I shall lecture
        on colostrum.

THIS IS NOT THE END OF MY FILM CAREER

Look, I may be no Meryl Streep, but unlike *that* Daughter of the Revolution, I do my own stunts. Wig or no wig, I'm gonna play the hell out this part. For example, in the first scene, they wanted grandma to break a hip, so I gave them a broken hip: I careened from kitchen counter, over stools, and fell precisely on my mark. People know when they are fooled, they want the real thing. Do you know what I told the director when the "firemen" chopped down the door to save poor old granny? I cannot work like this. They are too pretty to put out fires. I'll just lie here until you find the right type to carry me off screen. The child actors—like my very own children!—grew tired of the delays and shoved the food stylist's props into their mouths. It's the same thing for this extended nursing home scene. I told the director: look, the lighting in here is terrible, and there are so many characters at different hours, I'm not sure we even know what the story is anymore. I'll have to review my contract when my son comes in for his cameo. Did I mention my daughter-in-law wrote the script? She keeps revising it, but the ending's the same. Sure, I've heard the gossip that I'm being replaced by someone younger. One day, I'll just walk out the door and into a location with better exposure.

THE 11TH DAY OF OCCUPY WALL STREET

The State feeds on their anemia

—E.M. Cioran, *A Short History of Decay*,
translated by Richard Howard

1.

And my mother close to spending her last cent
on transfusions: which Edna St. Vincent Millay
likened to poetry translation. All the blood
sacks screened for bad habits,
classed by type—and not by
temperament—loosen an immigrant's
militance: a name
and a place of origin. My mother says,
this is a young person's
blood, I can feel it
rolling down
my thighs.

What if, in the most terrible collision, blood type
between mother
& daughter, between original
and copy, proves incompatible?
We prick each finger,
smear two glass slides,
and place them
on a text called the future.
A rejection of another's

into the crowd's
dark center, its leagues
of fingers.

They are
lost or expelled,
a lesson
taught.

3.

Although there's
blood in
this poem, that's not
the plot.

The plot is
money. Money's
the plot.

4.

I was a Wall St.
temp,
rose into
buildings
now gone or netted over—
I said
hello
as a corporation. Lost
calls, passwords,
wore the wrong

blood, a faulty translatior
won't necessarily
kill you. But your own blc
reintroduced
into your body
quite literally
is not
without its
dangers.

2.

A young woman with bel

Another with breasts
exposed to autumn
air: demands written on t
bodies, read
by a rush
of cameramen.

In the performance that is
that is being pretty
prettiness is currency
is capital
gain.

When the protest or para
turns ugly
both the pretty and the pl
lose their shirts,
chased or pulled

thing. I dreamed of marrying
myself
onto the main island.

Lovers were easy
as bike rides
through the park, a deck
of outcomes,
like assignments
or cubicles. One begins
to believe vigor
a résumé. Some nights,
I locked myself out
and climbed
the escape.

It was a place to lay my head or await a proper diagnosis.
Confused by my choices, I was told the slit in the skirt
would distract the traders, particularly the
Venezuelan, a diplomat's
son. "Finish faxing and pack up
your pumps."

We were a colony of temps
each sent to work
a parcel of land
as punishment
for our cheap taste.

5.

A shirt mooned with dye

and sweat
enters the kitchen.
This picture serves
as entrance into a
mind, the fake brick backsplash
the curvy mahogany cornice
over the sink. My father's face
at the threshold of
air-conditioning
handing his wife
a check.

They say dirty for gross pay
and clean for net.

My parents' passbook savings
stamped weekly by the neighborhood girl
who professed not to know
Spanish. I know who you are
my mother once told her
through the glass
partition.

Now all the money's gone. We lose
our name in its
absence.

Money
as autobiography.
As fairytale
mirror.

6.

The word overtime
astounds me now,
so far
from the old
measurements.

Also cash:
a wonder
a sonnet.

7.

I dream I've drugged my way
out of place. I've slept my place out of me.
    I announce to my students that this is the only way to where
    we are from.

I try to reconstruct the bodies, each,
but I confuse them,
I try to meet that thought.
I try to hear what it is. It's a chanting:
I rally the mob
    against my current body.
Someone in a Guy Fawkes mask carries
a sign denouncing
my many exuberances.
Now I'm on
to something.

A reporter flips open his notebook
and skips over me. No photograph
to accompany
my side, no record
of the story.

8.

I worked for coffee, sugar, & cocoa and learned the art
of the spit, levels of acidity, how to return things
a lady boss ordered
from the Home Shopping Network.
She also kept me waiting in the Women's section
of Bloomingdale's, and after I was educated
did time at Planned Parenthood
with posters of runaways and a baby
in a pinafore. I was then
reading Creeley.

That and the neurologist, you could say I was
out of pocket, in the sense the vibrations
ran through my legs and through
my privacies. One who sleeps in commercial
districts is regularly made public
and awakened
for repair. There was also the weird guy
down the hall who dragged
his trash down the stairs
and later held a hooker
against her will. Her name
was Rosa. True
story.

9.

On the phone my mother confuses
words. She hears worry inside
of story, a swift kick thundering
from sweet kiss.
Driving back from Canada years earlier
she wished her kids could sing
for her knee surgery. The notes I carried—
idle in traffic just that side of the border—
were rheumatoid. But what do I know
about melody, Ma—I'm an American, I need
images.

10.

In the great tradition of courtly love,
a modern day sonneteer sets out to serve
women engaged in the cause
and with his subtle and wistful lens
slows the lashes and mouth
as they open suddenly for him, the bony flex
of shoulder blades, hair fanning softly
near a tattoo. Every frame enjambs
to unfold one labile body
after another. Hope exits their mouths
as warm air.

And just to make clear
the powers they denounce
are inescapable
he names it

Hot Chicks
of Occupy Wall Street.

11.

I fold cash for the house cleaner
in thirds
and she tucks it
into her sweater pocket
as she tells me
about her car. Her son.
A bus trip back
home. We both
talk as if nothing has just
happened. I thank her for
all she's done.

12.

The drug or dare I took
was a bus daily
to push out into
some place, the someone
I might be.

The place now
the pushing
of someone
out of me.

After they've wiped
blood off

the baby
I know this place
is a dream
called money.

But money recedes
into the scenery
just as the scenery
grows greener
around me.

13.

My mother's early bedtime
closes the gap
on wakefulness, each day
shorter. "Democratic
awakening" turns
televised weather, a dim
forecast
from her mechanical
bed. Ask her about that hurricane
sweeping across the oil-rich
end of Texas
she imagines
me in.

NATURAL DISASTER: A DREAM

This is the secondary revision. A large window
to the ocean.

                        (I wanted to finish the book
                        about my mother
                        in an idyllic setting.)

This is the instant the wave curls toward the window
                        and the computer quietly trembles.

I say to my mother: I'm taking you upstairs
to be with your husband. Mother,

I'm wheeling you away
from the storm.

But she has forgotten what husbands
are for. I tell her they are to roll towels
under the door.

                        (For lunch we had squid. I cooked it to rubber.
                        It bounced from the pan
                        as power of attorney.)

The sky darkens and the town scrambles to empty. I know
this is my last chance to add
footnotes or a glossary.

Over the loudspeaker the absentee landlord
promises a helicopter. He assures us, "All the papers
are in order."

But it's a trick: he's lured me to his office
to collect the rent. And what to do
for lack of words
but show him
what it feels like
to drown. He looks unimpressed
as I suffocate my son.

This is the revision that rhymes. This makes sense of time.

MOTHER, MONSTER: A LECTURE

1.

On the Apulian red-figure kylix—a platter-sized cup
fashioned before Christ—Pasiphae frowns as she prepares

to nurse, yet again, a monstrous mistake. Minotaur,
with his beach-bound muscles and cologne-ad

chest, eyes us sideways from his shrunken bull-head, smirking
and satisfied: I mean, you want to send this little beast immediately

to the labyrinth. You want to lift Pasiphae's right hand
to catch a glimpse of his sex. Animal? Human? But dwell

on the striking ambivalence of the left hand, hovering
over Minotaur's barely formed horns. As a mother, you hope

it lands gently to stroke the calf's hide. But the look on Pasiphae's face
is a history of debts settled in neither woman's

nor child's favor. Also etched on the kylix is a pot, much like a slow-cooker,
and a swan. Here is a goddess meant to glide smoothly along,

not stay home to watch the roast. Still, she carries Poseidon's curse
to term and must hourly pull out her breast. As you study

her royal gown, look among the folds for slits, a pop-up advertises,
"New Sitter & Nanny Profiles. Added daily. Join Now!"

2.

In Pollock's "Pasiphae"—which some say he named
"Moby Dick" before persuaded to change

it—the thrust is the same: a lust so large for
white bull or leviathan that the body becomes

a tempest, its own imminent shipwreck, willing
to construct any vessel to near its longing. Romano

shows Daedalus guiding Pasiphae through an opening
in the wooden cow's hide, a flap that yields darkly

and easily like vaginal lips held apart
for a camera. She looks over her shoulder, perhaps

hoping she'll be talked out of it, but this is not
her own design and as she positions herself

uncomfortably into her bestial nature, the bull
is betrayed by his own. Masson in his drawings and paintings

satisfies our hunger for depiction of the act: up goes Pasiphae's
big toe in the air, her legs spread, as the white bull,

nose-flaring, gives it to her in ways that render
the page an afterimage of limbs shearing

through grass, a confusion among the heather.

3.

On wedding chests decorated with
highlights of the myth, the question of desire

—do we kill it or let it eat what it will—
is resolved for newlyweds: in the labyrinth Theseus

pierces Minotaur with his sword, and returns to Athens, sails
black but triumphant. But where in these scenes do we find

Pasiphae after news of her son's death? As she sits remembering
her belly stretched by the size of the calf carried

the typical nine months, the painful latch as she begged
for a wet nurse who would never come? Here, we'd say, she named

him not atrocity but Asterios, ruler of stars. Here, they stared
at each other—mother, monster. A maze long before any built.

And, here, she first pointed her nipple up, to release a string of milk
into his mouth.

QUESTIONNAIRE

Who has taken my place
and sits you

on the toilet? Who
lifts you from

wheelchair and puts you
to bed? Who

has taken my name
and married another,

sends her kids
to Catholic school,

and brushes
your hair? Who

comes in singing
with your tray, and

lovingly washes
your underwear? Who

has given me
an accent and

upper-body
strength? Who

has me decorating cakes
and remembers

your name? Who's
taped a picture of my

likeness to the wall? A stranger,
a darker face. Who

has taken my cats
and made them a dog? Who

shops there, not here,
for ground beef? Who

has made me one of
the gals? Who

has taken me
for immigrant? Who listens

to your weather reports,
believes in so much

catastrophe? Who's
riding the bus? Whose

name on the pass?
But for the grace, whose

work is closer in range to who
you were? I am busy at

nothing, my avatar
has come in

with a suspense
of pills in gel-filled

cups. Who
prescribes all those

drugs? The scripts
are impossible to read. Could I

have written them myself?

THREE

PROJECTION

As when we photograph
a room in our
since abandoned
childhood home

and stand
in the drugstore
trying to make sense
of a white presence

—striations of light
distinctly
human—

AND(U)MASSIVE

FLESHED

moving
towards the
window,

this brutalist
building
in Texas
develops
on its surface

the very thing
that possesses us
or at times

blows open
the curtains

on a still day

    who are our enemies

        too early to tell

We look
to an adjacent
roof

for some sign
or source
of projection

as when we tell
stories

to each other
of some uncanny
occurrence

WITH RAPE

today   p the South
                 e
                 o
                 p
                 l
                 e

                 o
                 f

13 Negro pupils

        summer White

a rattling
of the kitchen chair

that repeats
nightly

WHY?

and explain
it away

      "it is difficult, certainly,
      to go on scanty
            reports"

perhaps it was
the cat

or the house
settling
into its bones

REALLY DEFLECTING

But this presence
a quiver
at dusk

becomes fevered tulle
as evening
comes over us

a rush of rows
pierced by shafts

OIL

2,838.   **CRUDE**   **FUTURE**

the past
giving way to the
present
across a grid
of empty offices
that hold
and fabricate
the archive

and we ask

FOR WHOM?

OF whom?

are these ghosts

when there is
no one to witness them

They recede
then swell with

ACTI(CON)CERNS

ANOTHER

FLARE-UP

taken over by this
underworld

accumulations
of memory

and erasure

reports of the living

SECOND-MURDER STATE

and the dead

  "the rumor
  that has
  reached them"

spelling spilling
now

in similar patterns
of grammar

a national
haunting

   "the word we have"

and the law
which governs
us

As when we—
couple
and child—

stand
enclosed in the
university's
concrete plaza

MIDDLE

CLASS

spectators

and confuse
two homeless men

ECONOMIC (G)RAISE(ON)

at first
for enthusiasts
of conceptual art

as they walk past
and into
the lobby

we guess
to use the
restroom

How seriously do you find this civil rights
situation?

The guard exits
the building
for a coffee
break

w
e

c
a
n

s
e
n
d

o
u
r

m
e
n

o
u
t

and ghosts
of the archive

`bottom against its working`

multiply ever
steadily

The specter
of the missing boy
last seen walking
to the bus stop
rises over us

and we look
for our daughter

PERSONAL   **know**

who has
run off

balancing now
on a bench
unable to read

as yet
untroubled.

FOUR

TRACE OF LOVERS

1.

Boys in basketball jerseys
turn
    from the sneaker sale
        and elbow
            each other.
  They walk away
     & come back.

The breast drawn into
public view
by a good
latch.

All those hormones
dizzying
the horde
pull them
closer

to find a tiny mouth
wedded
to their desire

and
my belly
whose ancient scrolls
unfurl.

Is this not
what they
bargained for?

2.

What other animals
are awake
with us?

The cats hide beneath
their paws. The neighbor's
five dogs peaceful
at this opaque
and formless
hour.

A lizard's grey-pink underbelly
strobes across
the bathroom window.

Our bed
wild kingdom
our burrow.

You suckle me
into the dream of the tiger
running after the baby
antelope.

My brothers yell, GO! GO!
and I turn from the TV set

as wobbly-legged
he collapses into brush.

3.

The breast pump buzzes
   & beeps at intervals
  through my office door.

Their professor
perverse
madonna & machine
if suddenly they entered
with camera.

My body is penmanship
marginal
to their poems.

Why alarm them?

My rushed sign reads:
Do Not
Distu^b
  R

4.

The cacophony of mating season
on NPR.

Could a male penguin thaw
this bag of breast milk
between fat and fur?

> I cannot imagine sex in Antarctica.
> (I'm not to imagine sex
> at all)

5.

Halo of milk inside the bra cup.

The afterimage, the olfactoid.

A shroud
for the faithful. Who
is just one.

O, ye
of little faith.

6.

In the playground no one smells
on me the cumulative trace
of lovers. My milk, my ilk
as alibis.

But I want to confess
to fantasies filthier
than the baby pool.

Then a phobia,
a strange moral
tic.

The bra flap clicks
back into place.

7.

At the baby shower
she unwraps
and holds in the air
a Hooter Hider.

PARAMOUR

English is dirty. Polyamorous. English
wants me. English rides with girls
and with boys. English keeps an open
tab and never sleeps
alone. English is a smooth talker
who makes me say please. It's a bit of role-playing
and I like a good tease. We have a safe word
I keep forgetting. English likes
pet names. English
has a little secret, a past,
another family. English is going to leave them
for me. I've made English a set
of keys. English brings me flowers
stolen from a grave.
English texts me, slips in
as emojis, attaches selfies
NSFW. English has rules
but accepts dates last minute. English makes
booty-calls. English makes me want it.
When I was younger, my parents said
keep that English out of our
house. If you leave with that *miserable*,
don't come back. I said god willing
in the language of the Inquisition. I climbed out
my window, but always got
caught. English had a hooptie
that was the joint. Now my mother goes gaga
over our cute babies. Together
English and I wrote my father's

obituary. How many times
have I said it's over, and English just laughs
and says, c'mon, señorita, let's go for
Chinese. We always end up
in a fancy hotel where we give
fake names, and as I lay my head
to hear my lover breathe,
I dream of Sam Patch plunging
into water: a poem
English gave me
that had been given
to another.

GETTING AROUND THE SUBJECT

Ways that I avoid calling you: etymology, falling into a shallow ditch
and asking for a shovel. A blog: (insert here your favorite
de-clutterer).

What can you tell me about the ether that stripped you
from my birth, that tore you from you, as do
all calls to service?

Ways that I avoid hearing it straight from you: a photocopied
time table's breakfast bells, a shift
in river courses, other cues. Even music,
the silhouette of shoes
taped to the floor. I follow arrows and numbers and arrive
in someone else's arms.
Look here—*dip*—is
what it's like
to barter.
A cat (thought a hare)—*twirl twice*—skinned, from
the black market.

And then there's the system in which I aim all questions at you in the form
of answers. I commandeer the test site and also assist
the cheaters. What will you say
when results are in? Take me to the museum? Not
likely.

Ways that I avoid your practiced evasion: Cooking as if
divorcing my parents. Dear Reader, you know ways to
cut in half: sugar, salt, fat?   Spend the evening
                         listening to a temperance lecture. Or, bring
                                   down the china
                                   for the big idea visitor.

DEAR STRANGER

Our plane that night cut through sheets of ice, cleanly, and then through clouds. Close to the ground, the sheets turned thicker, the plane's engine started to cough, we sat there each edged in by the fear of death, and also the armrest. How does one survive desire for another, I asked you, to ease the tension. How does one survive these flights? The ice turned to sheets of paper, and as the plane ripped through them, they doubled in size. We read each moving sheet, which contained questionable instruction, I was not helpful and said they were poems. How does one survive the desire for big answers, and you grasped my hand as if I might leave. O, the mercy of the body, trying to out-run history. When finally we landed, our plane bullied its way through police cars, pedestrians, SUVs. And ahead of us, another plane curled into pieces. Here was our future, we shall rise as cones of smoke, our casings shall feather weightlessly to the ground. But you reasoned, "That's not us, they must've had a drop in pressure." We made it out and over monkey bars and down a slide, where we sat and waited. The papers were stuck to the plane, everything not said, my waste and the waste of others. And more words irretrievable in the overhead, as in the heart. Sometimes I imagine falling into the ocean with my seat cushion. The mercy of the body able to float, until it tires and gives in. It's funny that the best part is no longer having to swim.

PEDAGOGY: A DREAM

The woman swam interpretively from a school chair, the kind
that locks you in & allows you to write
or sit there
pretending to listen   Her arms, wing-like, triangled
from shoulder to wrist, then twisted into the air
as if clearing a space   The ball-joints rotating on question &
answer   I thought her skinnier and whiter and more American, verging
on Appalachian   Everything about her was sharp, she did not
exceed her limits, though her age hung
from her
armpits.

Was she my own project, did I see her as me,
being batty as they say of old women, getting ready to dive
into it fully as if the older body that awaits is of water and will
swallow and distort me and fill my ears with a physical
history, most likely my own? I put myself together
then pull myself apart
to reach for the other me in the wake.
                         And most striking:
                                    there was no audience or class
                                    and she sat in the back of the room
                                    focused on nothing
                                    but her perfect stroke.

TRAINING

To each train its compartments, to each man his foiled sandwich.
Typically of ham or Spanish omelet. Things that keep their seats,
as assignments.

What is your first memory of jealous lovers? Were you yourself suspicious
of others? Here they are as I remember them. My daughter nurses the tally:

My brother puts his fist through a door inches from Farrah Fawcett's stiletto.
My best friend writes an angry letter to her sister's boyfriend.
    She later calls me out, accusing me of treason. I become her twin
        often out of convenience.

A farmer stands in the train's corridor with his perfect tomatoes and
    shows them
to my mother. In his palm he slices one open for her, and sprinkles it
with salt. The salt draws the juice out.
    It is many towns and a long night for us. My father's imagination
    hybridizes
        into monster crops.

As if the memory of burning hairs from hooves or soaking tripe in vinegar might an enclosure make, traction from the present leads us back and not to the other side of the curtain where a woman wails to pry open a lid. We casually break off pieces of crackers and wipe on cheap napkins oil and anisette, until the middle child crosses the threshold, unafraid. We have failed in the most basic rule, to never turn from offal in favor of quiet or self-care or need, as if the ugliness and flavor of it would make unpronounceable our names. When we knew the secrets of transformation, of the long simmer, the cure, the careful pluck. Still, we fail every moment we turn our slippery grammars against us and let our children be adopted into perfect homes. We stood there, my brothers and I, ladling the honeycombed stomach into your dish, the last holders of something funny, yet never told again, as a cowlick fixed moments before the bulb flashes. We laughed that we knew the joke and were the joke but would fail the test of translation. For which our children groan and push away a dish and throw open the curtains, their sunshine so big and so original. What do you call it, when in a mind and in a language the sun goes down? When you float from floor to floor or let your sister braid your hair an afternoon before the war? "I leave and they don't know. To find a bed that is my own."

ARCHAEOLOGY OF VESTMENTS

I remember the fine pleats of your tunic, how they found you among the funerary rags. Your bicep, evident. The crease of your inner elbow. The perfect press that flattened each fold; a funny lie. You were wayward, you wallowed.

I remember pouring buckets of hot water onto ice until your body emerged. That you were preserved in your string skirt, hung low on the hips. Something alkaline made the threads rich, something made you kin.

I remember what you wore when there are now only words.

I remember how they chased you out of town in your own confection. A print unsuitable for marriage.

You wove and unwove, but you were no Penelope. You were my mother re-inventing English in her copycat fashion, and then you were a boy in a band whose ripped jeans I sold. And then you were a rack of babies, from which I stole one.

MISE EN GARDE

Danger the bird will bypass her cot
Danger of seeming nonchalant
Danger in knowing the spill of consumption
Danger in blood and its familiar trenches
Danger in anger and dangle and gerund
       gender and candy
       and absent grandparents
Danger we'll forget to tower the princess
Danger in hair that grows its assistance
Danger we'll parent with cultish fervor
Danger in Sears or Spock or Ferber
Danger in despots and kindly old ladies
Dangers that thrive in arid climates
Danger our daughter will never learn bus routes
Danger of the curb and the cars and the costumes
Danger her speech foreign to my own
Danger we'll mirror each other in tone
Danger of insistence spelled kin and existence
Danger my mother will shred the board's minutes
       (No one will know I was once one of them)
Danger of lobes puritan and savage
Danger we'll become like all the others
Danger the beautiful names of poisons:
       Aromatics, aromatics, all around us
Danger we'll crush her with identity theories
Danger it keeps us from watching a movie

Dangers at borders, in bars, and on boats
Danger in Idol & Survivor & Lost
Danger she'll beg us for the newest iPhone
       ("But, Mama, it's so boring on the moon!")
Danger in the endless Internet search:
Hot dogs=carcinogens=slow painful death.

VOICE: AN ESSAY

I believe in voice
as I do in ghosts.

Even Freud saw the ghost
of a dead patient
in his office:

"There is a grain of truth concealed
in every delusion."

When my friend died
his parents detected
in the sudden clinking
of the chandelier
his presence,
as if unexpectedly
he had returned
from college
to ask, "What's
for dinner?"
And they laughed
for the first time
in days.

"A voice is all that can cut
through it."

Soon after, his bereaved
girlfriend slept with his

brother, easily mistaken
as his twin.
Did they make love
as a way to speak
to him through
each other?

"They were right who inveighed against
the voice,
too sexual an organ"

Sometimes at night
a voice rises
from a set of
actions deep inside

"This wooing of another voice"
"a voice we cannot help listening to"

and in Spanish
pleads with someone
who can't hear me. It is as if
I have multiple mouths
and ears, inside
and outside of the dream.

I have also many lovers
in attics crowded
with costumes
and my father is alive
walking backwards
over a railing.

Jeff breaks the spell
calling me back
into the present
in English. He shakes
my arm and the voice retreats.

"A phantom can thus
be sensitive
to idiom."

I try to run toward my father
or close the hatch behind a lover
or simply fall back asleep.

"I do not sublimate
in the same way
in Chinese
or in French."

Freud relates
the story
of the apparition
in third person,
revealing only later
that he himself
had witnessed
the ghost.

Then, that the figure
was not a ghost
but a dead patient's
sister also afflicted
with Graves' disease.

The voice in the dream visits again
and again and is mistaken
as the same. Why does
it appear? To understand
a shared affliction? To take
the place of the dead
or air its concerns? I bet
the sister came to settle
the doctor's bill.

My grandmother
slept with the lights on,
her long grey locks tightly wound,
worried her dead husband
would return
to fulfill his final
threat:
"If you're not good to me,
I'll come in the night
and drag you out of bed
by your hair."

The ghost of my
grandfather
night after night
not as diaphanous figure
aerial and bellowing
but as a voice
that could conduct
in his wife's mind
a terrifying rehearsal.

Farid and I talk
not of ghosts
but of family stories
that possess us
and traffic bodies
through our poems.

"Mientras más violenta es la historia
menos hablan los personajes de sí, consigo,
con otros. Es un ritmo irrespirable."

I believe in poems
as I do haunted houses.

We say, someone
must have
died here. There,
there is a patched wall
where the bullet
exited the head.
We make sense of noises,
this one being
a noisy ghost,
by some fuzzy
tale the neighbors
tell in pieces.

"a tiny bit of an absent narrative"

We ask
questions into
abandoned rooms,

the answers
not apparent until
we play back
what we've taped
on our sensitive recorders
and listen agape
to voices rising
in waves and peaks.

Or, we try to conjure them
by moving our fingers
back and forth
over letters that spell
out exactly what we didn't
expect but take
as true. Or they keep
telling us NO, NO, NO
in jerky movements
of our wrists.

Voices, like ghosts,
always win. They can
walk through walls
or move furniture.

GHOST SONG

Three times on Saturday
I remember you
as dead,
mamá.

I reach under
my shirt
surprised
to find
the nipple dry,
surprised
there's something
left of you
an orange I section
in the sun
and hand to my
daughter.

The fight this morning
to part evenly
her hair.

Ghost milk
again on the nipple
as I make
the bed.

Bitters drained
from eggplant
black liquid
through a colander.

Bedtime is classic
matricide.

She touches
my nipple
through
pajama shirt
and sings
as Sappho
to her beloved:
"I like your beauty, beauty."

NOTES

"Dear María" assembles parts from Wikipedia entries on "Maria"; "Murder in Juárez: Gender, Sexual Violence, and the Global Assembly Line" by Jessica Livingston (*Frontiers: A Journal of Women Studies*, 25.1(2004): 59-76); *Migrant Imaginaries* by Alicia Schmidt Camacho (NYU, 2008); "Electrolux, other maquiladoras affected little by bloodshed in Mexico" by Ryan Jeltema, *The Daily News* (Michigan), 7 March 2011; and "Juarez maquiladoras recovering despite bloodshed" by Will Weissert, Associated Press (22 January 2011).

"Heritage Speaker" quotes two misremembered lines of poetry. The first is from Joe Brainard's poem, "I Remember," which reads in the original, "I remember waking up somewhere once and there was a horse staring me in the face." The second is from the Bernadette Mayer poem that begins, "First turn to me after a shower."

"My Body's Production" originated in Lowell, MA, where I researched textile factory work, thanks to a University Research Institute grant from the U. of Texas at El Paso. The italicized lines are from sources found in the library and archives of the American Textile History Museum (special thanks to librarian Clare Sheridan): *Spinner*, Volume IV (1988); testimony of Elizabeth Bentley, who had been a child laborer in a Lowell textile mill, quoted in *The Belles of New England: The Women of the Textile Mills and the Families Whose Wealth They Wove* by William Moran (St. Martin's Press, 2004); and a letter from Madge C. Gunn, textile worker in Lowell, to Mrs. Cora Hotchkiss (Feb. 1, 1874).

"Purity & Danger: A Performance" and "Mother, Monster: A Lecture" draw from "Nursing Mothers in Classical Art" by Larissa Bonfante, in *Naked Truths: Women, Sexuality and Gender in Classical Art and Archaeology*, eds. Ann Olga Koloski-Ostrow and Claire L. Lyons (Routledge, 1997), and "Masson's Pasiphae: Eros and the Unity of the Cosmos" by Doris A. Birmingham, *The Art Bulletin* (69.2 (1987): 279-294). "Purity & Danger" also pays homage to anthropologist Mary Douglas.

"Projection" was commissioned by the Landmarks Project at University of Texas-Austin. The poem interacts with Ben Rubin's media installation "And That's Just The Way It Is" (2012), which projected on the University's CMA Building in Cronkite Plaza a grid of overlapping and fluctuating text, drawn from live newsfeed and transcripts of news broadcasts from the Cronkite era. The poem culls text (arranged in the poem graphically) from one evening's projections, with additional texts (in quotes) from Cronkite's news report of President Kennedy's assassination.

"Archaeology of Vestments" pulls threads from *Woman's Work: The First 20,000 Years* by Elizabeth Wayland Barber (W.W. Norton, 1994).

"Voice: An Essay":

> "There is a grain..." and "A phantom can thus..." is from Jacques Derrida's *Archive Fever: A Freudian Impression*, trans. Eric Prenowitz (U of Chicago Press, 1996).
>
> "A voice is all that can cut..." is from Alice Notley's "Voice" in *Coming After: Essays on Poetry* (U of Michigan Press, 2005).
>
> "They were right..." is from David Shapiro's poem "Voiceless" (Lingo #4).
>
> "This wooing of another voice" is from Nathaniel Mackey's essay, "Cante Moro," in *Sound States: Innovative Poetics & Acoustical Technologies*, ed. Adalaide Morris (U of NC Press, 1997).
>
> "A voice we cannot help..." is from Barbara Guest's "The Voice of the Poem" in *Forces of Imagination* (Kelsey Street Press, 2002).
>
> "I do not sublimate..." is from Julia Kristeva's "The Impudence of Uttering: The Mother Tongue," translated by Anne Marsella (http://www.kristeva.fr/impudence.html).

"Mientras más violenta…" is from Valerie Mejer's poem "El desenlace," in *Rain of the Future/ Lluvia del futuro*, ed. by C.D. Wright, translated by A.S. Zelman-Doring, Forrest Gander, and C.D. Wright (Action Books, 2013).

"a tiny bit of…" is from Michel de Certeau's "Vocal Utopias: Glossolalias," translated by Daniel Rosenberg (*Representations*, No. 56, Autumn 1996).

ACKNOWLEDGMENTS

Poems from *MyOTHER TONGUE* first appeared in the following journals, blogs, and websites: *A Dozen Nothing, Bone Bouquet, Boston Review, Chicago Review, Cincinnati Review, Eleven Eleven, inactual, Mandorla, White Wall Review, WSQ,* Anna Maria Hong's posts for *The Best American Poetry,* The Poetry Society of America, and The Academy of American Poets.

They also appear in the chapbook *To the Archives* (Instance Press, 2014), edited by Elizabeth Robinson, and in the anthologies *The Volta Book of Poets* (Sidebrow Books, 2014), edited by Joshua Marie Wilkinson, and *Angels of the Americlypse: New Latin@ Writing* (Counterpath, 2014), edited by Carmen Giménez Smith and John Chávez.

A warm thanks to all the editors who, by soliciting and publishing my poems, encouraged me to keep writing.

Mil gracias to Futurepoem's Guest Editors Roberto Tejada and Mei-mei Berssenbrugge for selecting my manuscript for publication, and to Futurepoem's visionaries, notably Jennifer Tamayo, Dan Machlin, and Carly Dashiell, for making it into a book.

For their direct and indirect contributions to this book, I am grateful to my friends and colleagues in El Paso and elsewhere, especially Joseph Harrington, Farid Matuk, Forrest Gander, Andrea Cote, Jonna Perrillo, and Stacey Sowards.

MY LOVE & GRATITUDE

To those who cared for my mother in her mother tongue.

To those who care for my daughter on this fertile border between languages, lives.

To all the madres e hijas, especially Carmen Giménez Smith & Susan Briante.

To Jeff Sirkin.